ESPRIT DE CORPS

A Faith Building Encouragement for Police and Other Paramilitaries

Shantel C. Powell

ESPRIT DE CORPS. Copyright © 2023. Shantel C. Powell. All Rights Reserved.

Printed in the United States of America.

No portion of this book may be reproduced, stored in a retrieval system, or transmitted in any form or by any means, except for brief quotations in printed reviews, without the prior written permission of DayeLight Publishers or Shantel C. Powell.

ISBN: 978-1-958443-42-2 (paperback)

Scripture quotations marked "KJV" are taken from the Holy Bible, King James Version (Public Domain).

Scripture quotations marked (NIV) are taken from the Holy Bible, New International Version®, NIV®. Copyright © 1973, 1978, 1984 by Biblica, Inc.™ Used by permission of Zondervan. All rights reserved worldwide.

ACKNOWLEDGMENTS

My first debt is to a team of three women, Shevaughn, Kirsalyn, and Shanae, who were intentional about praying for me through the journey of writing my first book. I thought because the experiences shared where from daily encounters that, the process would have been smooth. Oh, was I wrong! I am therefore grateful for these ladies who were instrumental in me fighting the battle of retreating to my comfort zone.

Then there was the *Reach Million Author Accelerator Programme*, the birth place of this idea; thank you, Crystal, for your expertise and excellence. I am forever grateful for the insights and the pointed rigorous coaching system that you deploy—diamonds are truly formed under intense pressure.

I extend gratitude to Christopher. I remember the demands during the process got so overwhelming, and my environment was no longer conducive to my writing. I had to take a trip to the countryside to retreat and reignite the drive to get to the end. My brother, Christopher, opened up his home to me, and that was all I needed to write to the end.

To Cons. Rondon Thomas "T-Time", thank you for your unwavering support and assistance as a trusted colleague.

In the true essence of empowerment, God told me He started a good work and He can complete it (see Philippians 1:6). I saw His footprint along the way. He is the source of insights and gifted me with the ability and grace to write. Thank You, ABBA!

DEDICATION

Prayer pins us to purpose! For as long as I can remember, my mother has been saved. I am now in my late twenties, and I have never seen my mother leave her bedroom without reading her Bible and praying. Her consistency and walk of faith is an example for me to emulate.

My mother, a 70-year-old Christian veteran, has modeled Christ for me in every sense of the word. She has sacrificed her life for her children and lived to put them in a better place. Having attained some level of maturity, I realized from my late teenage years that she lived vicariously through me. Therefore, I now live with the intention to honor her. This book is my way of bringing my mother's passion and pride to the fore by encouraging others to engage God daily and find motivation in the mundane.

There is a group of people who never left the prayers of my mother; they are the civil servants—especially the police and soldiers—and this was long before Courtney and I became a part of this group. There is not a day that goes by that she doesn't pray for them. I, therefore, dedicate this book to them (specifically Cons. Rondon Thomas, a true fighter) from my mother through me, because no one models the thought that "prayer pins us to purpose" like she does.

TABLE OF CONTENTS

Acknowledgments iii

Dedication v

Introduction 11

Chapter 1: Fall In: Where Do I Stand? 13

Day 1: The Courage To Stand 15

Day 2: The Mind's Posture 17

Day 3: Getting Focused 19

Day 4: A Battle Of The Mind 21

Day 5: The Honour In Service 23

Day 6: Your Hands In His 25

Poem: 'Fight On' 27

A Call to Pray: That I Will Stand Regardless 28

Chapter 2: Faith Forged From Adversity: P.U.S.H Thyself 30

Day 7: Follow The Runner 33

Day 8: Check Your Source 35

Day 9: Know Your Place 38

Day 10: Shine Like A Star 40

Day 11: Xiao Lighthouse 42

Day 12: Wings Like Eagle 46

Day 13: If Strength were feelings 48

Day 14: No Perfect strength 50

Day 15: The Fabric Of Life 53

Day 16: Accept Help 55

Poem: 'Check Point' 58

A Call to Pray: Strengthen Me 60

Chapter 3: Weather the Weather 62

Day 17: Beyond Fear 66

Day 18: The Dirty Canvas 70

Day 19: Sugarcane Farm Visit 72

Day 20: More Than A Conqueror 74

Day 21: Find An Outlet 76

Day 22: The Dancing Sugarcane 78

Day 23: Slow Down But Never Stop Living 80

Day 24: The Eagle's Plight: Grace Your Pace 82

Day 25: The Brook Is Dried 84

Poem: 'Thou I Walk!' 86

A Call to Pray: Do Not Count Me Out 88

Chapter 4: The Commander's Voice 90

Day 26: Where He Leads 94

Day 27: The Wrong Right Turn 96

Day 28: Stand Still 98

Day 29: General Salute, Present Arms 100

Day 30: Fall Out 102

Poem: 'George' 104

A Call to Pray: Fight For Me 106

Chapter 5: Slow March 108

Day 31: Comparison Is A Thief 112

Day 32: Your Lane, Your Skills, Your Blessings 114

Day 33: One Hand Washes The Other 116

Day 34: How Much Can You Bear? 118

Day 35: My Energy Goes Before Me 121

Day 36: A Balcony View 123

Day 37: Impatience Thwarts Flow 126

Poem: 'Let The Science Speak' 128

A Call to Pray: Protect Me From Bad-mind and The Bad-minded 130

Chapter 6: Long Route: When Promise Meets Preparation 132

Day 38: This Confidence 136

Day 39: Let It Rain! 138

Day 40: You're Above Your Past: Make It Count 140

Day 41: Shake And Dweet 143

Day 42: The Dumpster 145

Day 43: Let The Rod Talk 147

Day 44: Serve And Grow: Impact And Go 149

Day 45: Talk Good 151

Poem: 'Preparation' 153

A Call to Pray: Be My Guide 155

Poem: 'A Note from Ribena' 157

About the Author 159

INTRODUCTION

As a young Bible-believing Christian, who has always been involved in church and church-based activities, the last thing on my mother's mind was that I would become a police officer. Her major concern was that I would lose faith in God because police do not get time to be with God and engage God as much as is needed.

I was swamped when I just started and needed to find a footing quickly. It was here I discovered that when you step out against the tide, expect the waves to rock your boat. Notwithstanding this reality, there is a call to weather the weather in order to achieve your goals and dreams and fulfilling your purpose. I am willing to do whatever it takes to stay connected. I am also extending an invitation to you to connect and stay connected.

Purpose is accomplished when there is an alignment with God and a connection to His truth and promises. As police and paramilitaries, the demands of our jobs limit our engagement with God and with faith-based activities leaving much to be desired in our devotion life. Here you get a chance to see that God is present everywhere and He is always talking and guiding. This devotional captures some of our day-to-day activities and packages them in a way that depicts the presence and involvement of God in our lives.

These experiences yield truth about God from a police and paramilitary perspective, and are packaged into seven chapters to shift your mind. You can engage God and maintain a good relationship by:

- Identifying where you stand.
- Finding faith is your adversity.
- Weathering the weather, whether you want to or not.
- Understand and appreciate the Commander's voice.
- Accepting your own lane (the concept of the slow march).
- Preparing for the promises.

We have what it takes to survive and thrive in godliness wherever we go.

"His divine power has given us everything we need for a godly life through our knowledge of him who called us by his own glory and goodness." (2 Peter 1:3 - NIV).

CHAPTER 1

FALL IN: WHERE DO I STAND?

The enemy on the outside cannot harm you unless there is an enemy on the inside. I have always wondered how I can restrict access to my peace of mind and emotion. How can we be confident in ourselves and our abilities so we know where we stand?

On July 11, 2021, I commenced training at one of the Jamaica Constabulary Force's training facilities. At about 6:30 pm, when we got settled and ready to rest, there came a loud sound, almost like an abeng beckoning us to convene. We did. This conversion was different. It required a set formation, and each person was positioned in a group, and each group had a structure. This structure depended on your unique traits, such as height, stature, or if you are able to lead. Everyone was positioned in a way that suited the intended arrangement.

So it is in life. We are suited for where we are meant to be because of what we have within us. This is what measures our ability to stand and determines where we stand. Therefore, it is important to become aware of what and who you are, when and where you stand, and what you have at your disposal. With God, we are able to stand and be counted because He who is within us is greater than he who is on the outside (see 1 John 4:4). An identity in God restricts and prevents the enemy on the outside from gaining access to our internal.

You are being called to assess your identity in Christ. The analogy of a "muster parade" and the dynamics of "falling in" in the appropriate order underscores how our uniqueness positions us for where we stand and what we do. It shows the importance of a source external to the group (a commander) that will help to shape the stance and order of the group, and this is where God is introduced as the source of our identity.

This first chapter has six days' worth of meditation and affirmation that will challenge you to appropriately fall in line with who you are and what you are positioned to do. The greatest restriction to our advancement is us: what we believe or fail to believe; what we do or fail to do.

DAY 1

THE COURAGE TO STAND

"The sovereign LORD is my strength; he makes my feet like the feet of a deer, he enables me to tread on the heights." (Habakkuk 3:19 – NIV).

The moment I realized I was called to stand, I knew this was not a one man show. I needed a support system that would never fail. I knew I needed God, and so do you.

Standing looks like taking one step in the right direction every day, taking responsibility for your actions or the lack thereof, committing to personal development, or bearing the weight of your purpose. Standing pulls on your entire physical and spiritual being, and this can be a debilitating thought. It is not for the weak, and neither is it for the strong. It is for you who know your strength comes from God alone. In the same way the feet of a deer are prepared for the terrains it must tread, so you are equipped to stand where you are called. You are equipped to stand because you have gone through all that you did. You are equipped to stand because what you have been through never claimed your life. Today, you are presented with a choice; to pull on the strength that God intentionally placed in you. Courage is doing it even though it is hard.

AFFIRMATION

My feet are prepared for the terrain I have to walk, and I have the strength to stand even though it is hard.

DAY 2

THE MIND'S POSTURE

"Now faith is confidence in what we hope for and assurance about what we do not see." (Hebrews 11:1 – NIV).

Being able to love means you have faith. Think about someone you love: a child, parent, spouse or friend. Ask yourself, "What wouldn't I do for this person?" There you go; you have successfully challenged yourself to see outside the scope of your reality. You just said, "I have confidence that I can do anything for the ones I love." If you just put that into action, boom! That is faith at work.

A reservoir of endless possibilities opens up when your mind is postured to accept the promises of God. The posture of your mind is responsible for faith, strength, endurance, and peace. You should actively guard your peace by checking what and who has access to it. Your mind's posture either limits your ability to advance or takes the limit off your possibilities. Your biggest dream remains out of grasp when your mind's posture is shaped by failure rather than the possibility of success. If you were to only think of what you can do for that loved one and never do it, what is the point? Confidence in the end goals should drive your action. Where is your mind in all of this?

AFFIRMATION

My mind is shaped by the possibility of success, and this gives me hope that if I continue to make strides—however small—in the right direction, I will remove the limits and unlock God's promises for me.

DAY 3

GETTING FOCUSED

"Let your eyes look straight ahead; fix your gaze directly before you. Give careful thought to the paths for your feet and be steadfast in all your ways." (Proverbs 4:25:26 – NIV).

You celebrate the victory that resides in your inner being that is awaiting the opportune time to be fully expressed. Until then, celebrate the little wins. Have you ever zoomed in on a photograph so much that you can see the pixels; the little units that create the picture? When you look at these units, it doesn't make sense that they are there, but if you should remove these units, the picture becomes woefully lacking. In the grand picture of victories, the small wins are the pixels. That is where your focus ought to be, and in moments when you feel like victory is out of reach, recalibrate your focus.

How many pixels have you already made? I recently learned this expression: "Yuh cya swallow cow and mek the tail choke yuh," which is translated: "You cannot swallow a cow and then choke upon its tail." This means the hardest part is out of the way, so you cannot allow the simple things to cause you to quit. The truth is, the simple things can cause you to quit if you have lost focus. As a teenager growing up in the country, I had to carry water from the community tank. This tank was down in a gulf, and the road was winding, cold, and rocky. I usually made pointers on the road to make the process more manageable. Though the aim was to get home with the water, the focus was to get to each point. The way to the end is to get to each point!

AFFIRMATION

I have the power to complete whatever I have started, and I give careful thought to my every action. The victory I seek is within my reach, and I'm taking it with full grasp.

DAY 4

A BATTLE OF THE MIND

"For as he thinketh in his heart, so is he: Eat and drink, saith he to thee; but his heart is not with thee." (Proverbs 23:7 – KJV).

My mind is mine. It is the motherboard for my being. As a man thinks, so is he (see Proverbs 23:7). If I am what I think, am I in trouble? Am I parading confusion and saluting a lie?

The façade of the century goes to keeping up appearance. There are three things that cannot stay hidden: the sun, the moon, and the truth. Who I am will surely surface. Will the real me be a disgrace? Take a minute to settle the score. What do you really think about? Is it serving you positively? You can perform to the audience of everyone else, but you cannot convince yourself to accept who you are not. The ongoing efforts to accept this falsehood have drawn a battle line. You remain at the front of that battle subjected to one of either two fates: if you accept the lie, you die; if you accept who you are, you silence the war in your mind. Will you live, or will you die? Accept that you are broken; you can be fixed. Accept that you have failed; you can try again. Accept that you have some scars; it means you are human. Accept that you cannot be perfect because no one is. Accept that if you are true to yourself, the internal war will cease, and on the other side of the war, there is peace. I am done battling me!

AFFIRMATION

Today I take charge of my mind. Positive thoughts in, negative thoughts out. I will repeat this as often as I need to.

DAY 5

THE HONOUR IN SERVICE

"Now that I, your Lord and Teacher, have washed your feet, you also should wash one another's feet." (John 13:14 – NIV).

If you serve yourself alone, you live for yourself alone and die a waste. Life is a puzzle, and you are only one piece. Our primary duty here is to serve others. Imagine if everyone's face was reflecting your image, that is, you see you every time you see someone else? How would that affect you serving them?

The heart of a servant must see that who you are called to serve is as you as they could get; emotional being subjected to the same frailty.

The eagle is the most majestic bird, but there is a time when it encounters danger and must be in a cleft until it is whole again. While in recovery, other eagles tend to and serve it until it is up again. If the roles are reversed, that eagle has the responsibility to serve another. We never think we will ever be in recovery, and this affects how we relate to others. While we are not serving to be served, we must consider the time when we will need to be served. We are linked to each other in this life, and shared responsibilities keep each of us alive and living. The honor in this is that you strengthen the hand of the weak, you extend grace unfounded, and you cover the vulnerability of those you are serving. There is honor in safeguarding the dignity of others, and, as my mom would say, "One hand washes the other."

AFFIRMATION

Who I serve is an extension of me; there is honor in extending myself to others.

DAY 6

YOUR HANDS IN HIS

"I will go before you and will level the mountains; I will break down gates of bronze and cut through bars of iron." (Isaiah 45:2 – NIV).

Sometimes the path you are called to take appears very unenticing, but we walk by faith and not by sight. Make the first step regardless. God has already made provision for every step you take in faith.

At 18 years old, I left home in the country to attend university in the city of Kingston. For a moment, I thought it was farfetched, but I was determined to change my reality, so I pushed the limits. Why was I confident to push the limits? I had my hand in God's. Having been backed to a wall by lack and cornered by the reality of hopelessness, I blindly made a step toward what I wanted and placed all my trust in God. I acquired a scholarship that was renewed every year for the four years of my study. You will not know how much God can fight for you if you have nothing to fight for. The mountains in front of you are what God promised to level. His designed route for you is laced with sensors of favour that are triggered by faith, which is expressed when you put your hands in His and just move.

AFFIRMATION

I just need to move!

POEM: 'FIGHT ON'

A day of peace I see
   Not the absence of war but the presence of the assurance that
It will be alright

Not all right, but certainly all is not wrong
Until the sound of the war cry ceases
I will sing my song
Faith forged from adversity,
Less is more; the weak is strong
Fight on, fight on!

Focus fixed, prize in sight
Rather to be righteous than to be right
Goals in view, morals held tight
Darkness present, but my mind is on the light
Where positivity prevails, bad energy takes flight
Present looks dim?
Your future is bright
Keep your head up child, my simple plight
Fight on, child
It's by His Spirit anyways and not your might.

A CALL TO PRAY:

THAT I WILL STAND REGARDLESS

Heavenly Father, creator of heaven and earth and the chief artist behind the masterpiece called mankind. You are acknowledged as the one who still holds the blueprint of my life and for that I thank You. Many times I question where I stand, who am I and find myself caught between the opinion of others and the truth of Your Word. Today, I pray for Your grace to accept what You say about me. I am he who You have called before conception and have mantled with a purpose to shake this earth.

I am he within whom You have placed the treasure of the Holy Spirit, giving me the power to chart a course of success in service, to have confidence in the expression of my God-created self, to demonstrate strength in the face of adversity, to have hope amidst despair, to muster courage to keep going when life wants to count me out and to find peace in Jesus even in the midst of chaos. I am he You have a plan for, a plan of prosperity, hope and a future.

I am protected from harm and my life is safe in Your hands. Help me to define where I stand so I can have the grace and the courage to stand with a mind's posture that taps into Your promises without failure. I pray that I am not distracted by the scheme of the enemy to put my life on pause, but I am focused and winning the battle in my mind. Therefore, I will be honoured in service, my life is in Your hands, and I have the guts and the grits to fight on in Jesus' name. Amen.

CHAPTER 2

FAITH FORGED FROM ADVERSITY: P.U.S.H THYSELF

I have the power to complete whatever I have started. The urge to quit will always feel better than the motivation to continue. So, it is the "how badly do I need to get this done" attitude, coupled with the required discipline to push and P.U.S.H that will keep you going.

The themes in this chapter are separated into four categories stemming from the acronym P.U.S.H (Persevere amidst the challenges, demonstrate Understanding, exhibit Strength and be Humble). If you learn this one lesson: "Don't stop when you are tired, stop when you are done," there is no telling what you can accomplish in this life.

I left my job in teaching to pursue law enforcement with a specific interest in Forensics. I knew this was going to be a rough ride and, trust me, I was ready for it, or so I thought. When the rigors of training set in, and bouts of doubt started to jab at me; when the sea of risk associated with being a police overwhelmed me, and the weight of under-compensation pulled me down, I remembered I started with the intention to win. Contrary to popular beliefs, winning is not only measured at the end. Winning is seen in every challenge you overcome. Every time you resist the urge to give in, it is getting up every day and wanting something so badly that nothing can stop you from getting it.

Adversity comes as a direct threat to your destiny and, if you allow it to have its way, it will cut you off from your God-promised inheritance. However, there is beauty in adversity. When you overcome them, your faith grows and prepares you to overcome those to come. The faith forged from adversity is fortified. It is graced, and that faith is rewarded. If you start, you will finish. Just start! Here are ten days' worth of faith-building encouragement as you push and P.U.S.H yourself.

PERSEVERANCE

DAY 7

FOLLOW THE RUNNER

"The end of a matter is better than its beginning, and patience is better than pride." (Ecclesiastes 7:8 - NIV).

No one knowing he/she has a life-defining race fails to prepare. Perseverance is indeed a measure of your ability to complete whatever you have started. It is broken down into two parts: how far you can go and how much you can take.

Ask yourself, "How far am I willing to go for this? How much can I take as a result of this?" Truth be told, we all want the end result, and if we could get there without having to go through the middle, oh, what a joy. But would it be a joy when you are not processed by the proceedings in the middle to deal with the end?

The middle is the second phase of preparation as it sets the tone for what is to come. The end will revert you to ground zero. There is a blessing in the middle and the end hits differently when you have not skipped the middle. For the runner, they discover strategies, find confidence, develop courage, find companionship, and forge life-defining relationships in the middle. They discover self in the middle. You find your limits and craft means to push boundaries in the middle. You develop resilience in the middle. The middle prepares you to show up and deliver. What can the runner do if he does not do the necessary work to perform? What can you do if you skip the necessary preparation? You will go through the middle because it is what will keep you standing. The darkness of preparation is the light that keeps your purpose lit.

AFFIRMATION

Better is the end of a thing than the beginning; I will not stop until I get to the end. I embrace the process because I was made to finish and finish well.

DAY 8

CHECK YOUR SOURCE

"Therefore encourage one another and build each other up, just as in fact you are doing." (1 Thessalonians 5:11 - NIV).

The middle tells you what works for you and what doesn't. I am a proud owner of an Andis T-liner that I used to give my clients a proper outline that is captivating. I have used it at two different locations, and I noticed that the T-line does not produce the same quality of work in both instances. This became a cause for concern, so I stopped to investigate. I found that on one occasion, the power supply was higher and adequate to power the machine. Therefore, I was able to produce a sharp crisp line and get a beautiful finish in a quicker time. In the other instance, the machine was barely cutting, and what should have taken ten minutes was taking thirty minutes of tedious work that was overbearing for both me and the client. I now understand that sources of electrical output carry different voltages, and devices and machines function at optimum when they are connected to the sources with their voltage specifications. Low voltage will cause your device to under-perform. It reduces productivity and quality, and will eventually destroy it. High voltage will burn it to naught. People are sources of output, and you are devices. What sources are you connected to? David's connection with his friend Jonathan allowed him to function optimally (see 1 Samuel 18:1-5). You are a source, so what are you outputting? As believers, we ought to be outputting love and not hate, peace and not war, patience and not anxiety, hope and not despair, faith and not fear. Perseverance is a measure of how far you can go. You cannot get very far with poor sources.

AFFIRMATION

I am unstoppable because I am connected to the right sources. I create an ambiance of love.

UNDERSTANDING

DAY 9

KNOW YOUR PLACE

"Pardon me, my lord," Gideon replied, "but how can I save Israel? My clan is the weakest in Manasseh, and I am the least in my family." (Judges 6:15 – NIV).

One of the dynamics of a good parade I took note of was the fact that everyone was strategically placed. Each person had an assigned responsibility, and these could not be performed from anywhere. The world is in chaos today because too many people do not know where they fall or they do know but they are busy trying to fit in the place of others. You may find that functional people give up on life, work, relationships, or just about anything because they are unsatisfied and unfulfilled.

You become unsatisfied and unfulfilled when you are out of place—you are a misfit. This life teaches you to be a misfit but still perform in the name of flexibility. Lies! If you must reach the end, you must understand and appreciate your place.

Gideon was a boy from humble beginnings who had no idea he had might and valor in him. He was tending to his father's pagan worshipper's herd. He let go of that which was not calling out his strength, that which told him indirectly that he had no place of value in this life. He decided he needed to get to the end of this challenge ahead of him, and he started by cutting loose of that which was not serving that purpose. Your purpose is as good as your ability to recognize that you belong here, and no one can take your place in executing your purpose. When you know this, shine from where you are. The power of knowledge is that wisdom preserves those who have it.

AFFIRMATION

I have a place here, and I will get to the end of my purpose. I hereby relinquish that which is not serving my purpose. It is okay to let go.

DAY 10

SHINE LIKE A STAR

"But we prayed to our God and posted a guard day and night to meet this threat." (Nehemiah 4:9 – NIV).

A star does two things; one is obvious, and the other is latent and consequential. It gives light, so without trying to be seen, it is noticeable. This light can be blinding, and this is consequential to the perspective of the onlooker.

You have one job, and that is not to be worried about who is being blinded by your light. Your sole duty is to shine. I had a dream once that I was going to be lost in this system by the powers that be. When I got my initial posting, I really felt lost in a remote place known best as bush-mount. One morning God reminded me that a light cannot be hidden, and this recalibrated my focus to my sole purpose, which is to shine from where I am by doing what I needed to do. What do you need to do?

Nehemiah built amidst the disappointment, discouragement, demotivation, and abject opposition of forces such as Sanballat and Tobiah.

Interestingly, note that once there is light, what is in the darkness will be revealed. Note that moths are equally attracted to light as those who need the light. Light affects three categories of people; those who love light, those who are in darkness, and those who want to cover the light. Guard your light! Sanballat and Tobiah affected the work of Nehemiah because they had access to him; they were those who should be helping him. Who has access to your switch? They could not hurt his work because he was internally wired with the confidence that the God who started a good work in him would complete it. Are you so wired?

AFFIRMATION

A star never stops shining. Today, I take back access from the light-breakers and tap into the wired confidence of God.

DAY 11

XIAO LIGHTHOUSE

"In him was life, and that life was the light of all mankind. The light shines in the darkness, and the darkness has not overcome it." (John 1:4-5 – NIV).

I was on mobile patrol one day and driving through a section of the Worthy Park Estate canefield when the driver shared an experience that shifted my mind from the patrol for a moment. The story was about how a light post guided them to safety. They were on patrol one night when they saw an unknown car driving through the area. They indicated to the driver to pull over; however, the driver turned on a section of the road through the canefield, and the patrol team gave chase. The poorly lit canefield was dark, big, winding, and creepy and could get anyone unfamiliar with the area lost.

The suspicious vehicle evaded the police by switching off its light in the canefield. The police were now left with one job; to find their way to the main road. Oh boy, was that difficult. To their rescue, they saw a streetlight in the distance. They followed the trail leading to the light and found their way out of the dreaded canefield. It was quite an experience for them, but it plunged me into deep reflection. Many of us are losing our conviction to shine because we don't see the immediate effect. Your light is the life that will strengthen the dying. This story reminded me of a few things that gave me reasons to keep shining:

- Light cannot be hidden.
- Shine, regardless of the naysayers.
- The world is still a dark place, and people need light. Your gifts and talents are needed, and it is still important for you to walk in your purpose.
- There are persons whose lives depend on you, at home, at work, or even at school.
- You cannot give up when the process gets blurred. Reposition and keep going.
- Light is life.

There are many reasons not to shine or be the best at what you find yourself doing, but none of it is an acceptable justification. When everything around you is bad, be the different one; be the one to bring peace in the midst of war and order in chaos. You be the light, be different and shine.

AFFIRMATION

It takes just a little light to pierce the thickest of darkness. I am that little light. I am a xiao lighthouse.

DRAWING STRENGTH

DAY 12

WINGS LIKE EAGLE

"He gives strength to the weary and increases the power of the weak. Even youths grow tired and weary, and young men stumble and fall; but those who hope in the Lord will renew their strength. They will soar on wings like eagles; they will run and not grow weary, they will walk and not be faint." (Isaiah 40:29-31 – NIV).

Look around you. Who is the strongest person you know? I am pretty sure of two things: you did not look within you, and you called this person strong because you have witnessed directly or indirectly this person going through some life-threatening challenges but managed to still stand. You would not think a person who exhibited vulnerability, who has openly broken down or succumbed to some challenges strong.

Sometimes we misconstrue the love of God as a reward for our faithfulness and the prize we get for keeping up an appearance of being strong. While God honors sacrifices and honors faith, He also holds up the hands of the feeble and strengthens the weakened knee. True strength lies in understanding your weakness and being able to push the limits by tapping into the everlasting reservoir of strength that is in God. It is this source that provides the strong with the stick-to-it-iveness they openly display amidst challenges.

Dependence on God is responsible for the strength you see and, by all means, that is what will also help you display the same. You shall rise up on wings like an eagles. Have you considered the majesty of an eagle? Strength is 'going' when everything around you suggests that you stop.

AFFIRMATION

I will stop at nothing, not even my limits, because wings like eagles are my aim.

DAY 13

IF STRENGTH WERE FEELINGS

"When you go through the waters, I will be with you;" (Isaiah 43:2a – NIV).

Stop fighting feelings; fight the source of the feelings. If you continue fighting feelings, you are engaging in an inconsistent battle; feelings are fleeting. Consistency gets you to the end.

"I don't want to have this conversation right now; I don't feel like it."

"My assignment is due, but I don't feel like doing that now."

"I know I need to mend that relationship, but I don't feel like it."

"I sense a call on my life but, hey, I don't feel like it."

"I know this must be done, but I don't feel like doing it."

"I am tasked to do this, but I don't feel I can manage."

If your feelings separate you from the purpose and responsibilities you are called to, then that is a direct attack on your progress. This is where you should target. There can be no display of strength if you are moved by the current of your feelings. Counteract these feelings with this age-old affirmation: *"I can do this because Jesus gives me strength."* This doesn't only nip the attack in the bud; it shifts your reliance from yourself and puts it in the everlasting reservoir of strength. If strength were in how we feel, we would all be weak. God is with you through the stages; that is strength.

AFFIRMATION

I may not look like I am fighting because I'm not leading a rebellion or shouting at the top of my lungs, but I fight by simply deciding to face the prospect of today even though I don't feel like it. I can do this because I have divine backative and support.

DAY 14

NO PERFECT STRENGTH

"That is why, for Christ's sake, I delight in weaknesses, in insults, in hardships, in persecutions, in difficulties. For when I am weak, then I am strong." (2 Corinthians 12:10 – NIV).

One of my high school teachers shared a quote with us in devotion one morning: "Write your goals in pen but write your strategies in pencil." At first, I said, "Wow, that's cool." It means your strategies can change, but your goals must remain. I did not read into the underlining and more important meaning of the expression: no process is too perfect that it cannot be affected by changes.

The process is strategically laced with unplanned realities to pull on the adaptability of the human spirit. The truth is, you will fall sometimes, but you must rebound. Your faith muscles are being flexed. God is not looking for perfect strength; He is looking for a commitment to do better at the next opportunity. If you falter, you don't have to fail because He uses everything, even the ones that don't make sense. He is the perfect strength in our imperfect vessels.

AFFIRMATION

Just when I thought I was done and out, I now know I can't stop because I am tired or weak. I will stop when I'm out. I have the power to complete whatever I have started.

BEING HUMBLE

DAY 15

THE FABRIC OF LIFE

> "For by the grace given me I say to every one of you: Do not think of yourself more highly than you ought, but rather think of yourself with sober judgment, in accordance with the faith God has distributed to each of you." (Romans 12:3 – NIV).

The basis of humility is understanding who you are and where you are at and accepting your limitations and imperfections. Humility is the submitting of one's authority to another because you now see him/her as important as you are.

My mother was seen as one the poorest members of our congregation while we were growing up. She had the most children, had no family business or children in any big job. Her sole income was from vending. I remember on one occasion the lady's fellowship was doing a fundraiser surrounding the theme "Grow your talent." Each lady was given some money to invest and get returns on. Mom took that money and bought some cane, took it to the market for sale, and made a profit. She continued doing this until she raised a good return on her talent. There were others who didn't do as well as she did because they were never in a position where they had to "turn their hands and make fashion."

In the fabric of life, every man is a yarn, and every yarn is needed. In the puzzle of life, every part is functional regardless of its size and stature. Most people will persevere. They demonstrate understanding and will find strength, which is great, but the buck is still stuck. The truth is, there are times when you must pull on others to advance to the next level. Tap into the ability of others; this is the hallmark of humility. You can go so far so quickly walking alone, but you will go miles further walking and working with others. Humility is the heart of teamwork, and the fact that you are humble doesn't mean you will always have the answers. Humility starts with accepting the humanity in everyone, valuing their importance, and not undermining their efforts.

AFFIRMATION

I am a part of the fabric of life as much as others are.

DAY 16

ACCEPT HELP

"Carry each other's burdens, and in this way you will fulfill the law of Christ." (Galatians 6:2 - NIV).

It is latent pride to believe you are the only one who is helpful and you can do without the help of others. I once had a dream about someone I look up to as a leader. In the dream, this individual was sick to the point where he had to leave his duty after asking someone to cover for him. I got up the next day with the dream resting on me heavily, but there I was saying, *"Oh, he is my superior. I'm not going to check in. I'm not going to blur the line of professionalism by getting personal."* Could I get through the day in peace? About 3 pm that day, I mustered up the courage to check in. The conversation went something like this:

"Hello, how are you?"

"I'm okay. What's up?"

"Very well. ☺ *Just checking in.*"

"Okay. I appreciate the check in."

"No problem."

Was I expecting him to be sick? Not at all, but I couldn't shake the feeling I was having, and with the resistance I came upon, I did not probe. The following day, he sent me a voice note asking me to do something for him. He did not sound well or okay. I did not hesitate to comment on what I heard. I said, "But you sound sick, man." He was very sick and was at a medical facility when I messaged him the previous day.

"I knew it was rather unusual that you would have been on my mind so strongly yesterday. That's why I messaged, but you said you were okay."

"Lol, I was at the doctor at that time. I don't like to complain. I'm well strong."

"Respectfully, that doesn't define strength. We should open ourselves to be consoled when needs be. I understand that people are averse to being vulnerable, but there are those who genuinely care and would want to express same. I don't view it as complaining; it's giving credence to our humanity."

On the journey of life, there are rest stops, and these are not for those who are not tired or worn. They are there for those who get tired, flustered, and weary as a means provided to replenish your strength so you can travel on. Humility is accepting that you need these stops every now and then, and that is okay.

AFFIRMATION

If I accept the help I need, I don't have to consider the question of giving up. I have the power to complete, and a part of it is the will to ask for help. I will not stop because I'm tired. I'll stop because I'm finished.

POEM: 'CHECK POINT'

Maturity is not faith
Faith is going against the odds
It's standing up for what you believe in
when everyone else would dodge
If it's not forged from adversity, is it really faith that you have?
Here I stand with plumbline.

Sitting, standing or waiting at the checkpoint
But check this point, keep your eyes open or they'll check your points
1, 2, all 3 of them;
You see people's vehicles rolling on to the check line
Be wary of those who send off the check lights
The bell, the book, and the candle
No adversity that comes upon you is too much for you to handle.
I stand with the plumbline.

Dark, dreary weather
Rolling tides, wailing billows
Sunken eyes, blissful sorrows
Amidst the weeping willows
I went in head straight, didn't care to know the sign
Oh, boi!
If faith were to be the result of the test time

I would have failed 90 and 9
But I can hope that it will be better around this time
Here I come with the plumbline.

In a world where people cease to measure how far they have truly come
You make sure as oft as is necessary, you hit that button and let your internal audit run
You can't go farther than your integrity will allow
You won't advance beyond the limit of your trust
Though the tides cause your moral fiber to be stretched
That is the only light
You really don't want to bite the dust
When I stand with the plumbline.

Yes, faith it till you make it
P.U.S.H thyself but never forget
Faith will sometimes break it
Shatter your mature decisions
Relentlessly challenging where you stand
At a checkpoint, around a podium, in your home
In a crowd or in the company of an audience of one
There you'll find a plumbline in my hand.

A CALL TO PRAY:

STRENGTHEN ME

God, You give the strength to the weary and increase the power of the weak but I don't always feel Your strength or feel empowered by You. Especially in times when all around me feels shaken and I feel broken, when there are needs to be met and the resources are scarce, when the war on the inside is going into overdrive and I feel to call a quit on life, when silent battles are not being won and the silent cries become even faint. But I am still hopeful that You can grant me strength so I confess my iniquities to You. I have failed to trust You as my source and I have without caution drifted from Your truth by believing the lies spoken over and to me.

Give me the grace to open up the darkest places in my heart and mind to You and give way to Your wind of peace. May Your oil of healing flow into the crevices of wounds I have craftily concealed. I now pray that my battles will end the way they should, and I will learn faith even from my adversities. By Your grace, I refuse to go under or to be overwhelmed by the silent cries that are growing louder. By You grace, Lord Jesus, I am a true example to my family, colleagues and the community.

I pray for the spirit of excellence in all I do, that whatever my hands touch will yield mind-blowing success. I pray that my strength will no longer be swayed by my feelings, but I will trust You as my perfect strength. I, by Your grace, accept Your help, GOD, to lead an exemplary life in my walk, talk and conduct, in Jesus' name. Amen.

CHAPTER 3

WEATHER THE WEATHER

"Weather the weather, whether you want to weather the weather or not."

I was in high school when this thought came to me. I wrote it down and, for what it's worth, I believed it to the point where it became a personal tagline. When you see me, know that whatever I am going through, I am going to get through it whether I want to or not. The essence of this expression is that it is an encouragement never to give up. I want that to be your takeaway from this chapter.

In January 2018, I lost my father in a tragic accident, and this interrupted and disrupted my life. I was placed in a situation to weather the weather, whether I wanted to do it or not. The truth is, there were days when my sails were broken but in those times, I learned that God is present in these seasons as much as He is when all is well. This chapter underscores the idea of staying on course, even when all evidence is pointing towards derailing you. Can you find and maintain peace in the face of unexpected situations such as disappointments, death, losses, and betrayal?

Over the next nine days, these devotionals will take you through three phases. Phase one is the pre-game plan and contains three points that prepare your mind to face whatever lies ahead. The greatest preparation is building on a God who cannot fail. With this confidence, there is no trial that will come that you cannot overcome.

As you navigate these phases, you will see where your preparation meets your expectations. When you prepare to execute, you can see yourself in a situation and see how you will get out. In this pre-game phase, you can see that beyond fear is everything that you expect—things that would keep you from stepping out—but there is also a part of God that you access when you move past fear. You will find that you cannot be too messy for God to create something beautiful with your life, and there is nothing that has happened in your life that God will make go to waste.

Phase two is the en-game phase. What do you do when you are going through whatever it is that has captured the attention of your emotions? When my father died, I rested on the promises of God and affirmed myself with His truth when the journey got really hard. It is important to remember that you are allowed to be human, to truly express how you feel, and work through these emotions with hope. Our job as police and paramilitaries is high risk and we have death among us arguably more than any other organization. The truth is, we are expected to still function. Since it is so, we can apply strategies that keep us going amidst all.

The third and final phase is the post-game phase. While settling into the new new, the event of adversity will cause changes in your life, and adapting to these changes is very hard. This is where many give up. Know this, it is okay to slow down but never stop. Grace your pace and assess your environment. This will dictate your next step.

Better is the end of a thing than the beginning (see Ecclesiastes 7:8). It is never how you start or where you start from; it is the finishing that counts. Will you finish strong?

Use these next nine days to build stamina as you weather the weather.

GOING THROUGH

DAY 17

BEYOND FEAR

"I will go before you and will level the mountains; I will break down gates of bronze and cut through bars of iron. I will give you hidden treasures, riches stored in secret places, so that you may know that I am the LORD, the God of Israel, who summons you by name." (Isaiah 45:2-3 – NIV).

The only way to get over fear is to immerse yourself into that which makes you fearful. Fear dwells on uncertainties (not knowing what will happen on the other side of your stepping out). For what it's worth, here are some things that will happen:

- Challenges, attacks, roadblocks, and even setbacks.
- You will lose what you don't need, even if you do think you need them—some mindsets, people, partners—but don't worry, God does not use what you have lost.
- You will receive alignment of people, processes, partnerships, and sponsorship.

- You will have success. You activate the hand of God when you move against the grain by faith, and whatever your hand touches, it is blessed.

Let's consider the fear ratio—the prospect of challenges over the possibility of success. Does your prospect of challenges outweigh the possibility of success? If your answer is yes, might I suggest this: you will get over fear when you have gotten under faith. Faith shifts your perspective by highlighting the promises of God. These are what God has promised:

- He will go ahead of you.
- He will level mountains.
- He will break down gates and cut through bars.
- He will give you hidden treasures and riches that have been stored in secret.

Why aren't you moving? Beyond fear is where you see the hand of God differently and, with each challenge, God has already strategized how He will walk you through it. (He has provided a way of escape; He is the way of escape).

AFFIRMATION

God goes before me, so every mountain is leveled, gates of bronze are broken down, and every iron bar that stands between me and success is cut through. He has provided the resources I need to get through: the money, people and support.

OVERCOMING

DAY 18

THE DIRTY CANVAS

"Come now, let us settle the matter," says the LORD. "Though your sins are like scarlet, they shall be as white as snow; though they are red as crimson, they shall be like wool." (Isaiah 1:18 – NIV).

I was watching a video on a barbering channel. A barber was transforming a man who had not cut his hair in a long while. The barber gave an advice that grabbed me. He said, *"Never work from a dirty canvas because it will not give you the desired finish."* I pondered it and said to myself, *"That is so perfect in the realm of barbering, and that's something I will always consider."* However, I know a creative who works from a dirty canvas and, in fact, He is the Chief of all creatives—God. He is the only one who takes you as you are; dirty, messed up, broken, scared, and imperfect. Going through and overcoming will get you dirty and messed up but know this, you cannot be too far gone from the grace of God.

In this life, there is so much pressure to be right and perfect that we miss the gift Christ wants to give us freely—His perpetual unconditional love that does not condemn but convicts. If you feel like a dirty canvas, maybe because of abuse, trauma, doubt, past and current involvements, make a move towards God, the chief creative, and the only one who works from a dirty canvas.

AFFIRMATION

If it's dirt, it's dirt, but I am certain I am not condemned. I'll accept the invitation to make it right.

DAY 19

SUGARCANE FARM VISIT

"When you pass through the waters, I will be with you; and when you pass through the rivers, they will not sweep over you. When you walk through the fire, you will not be burned; the flames will not set you ablaze." (Isaiah 43:2 – NIV).

God will take everything in your life that is classified as dirt and use it as preparation for the master art piece He is creating in you. God wastes nothing! This reminds me of a visit I made to the Worthy Park Estate where they manufacture sugar, among other things. The sugar cane is the primary raw material for this process. Here is what happens with the sugar cane: the leaves are burnt, and they fall back to the earth as fertilizers; the trash that remains after grinding the cane is used as bagasse which is very good for chicken coops and cleaning oil spillage in a garage, the juice gives us sugar crystals, rum, and molasses. Nothing is wasted!

I was so amazed by the whole process and began sharing it with a friend of mine. She asked, *"So, doesn't the char and soots from the burning affect the appearance of the product?"* I smiled because the answer is no. The product is clean and fair to look upon and to be desired by those who wouldn't even want to get involved with the process. The truth about God's grace is that when it is through with you, you will not look like what you have gone through. Weather your weather today because, as the manufacturers at Worthy Park make use of the entire cane, the chief manufacturer is making sense of your whole experiences; the losses you have faced, the mistakes you have made, the betrayals you have undergone, the bad decisions you have taken, the conspiracy against you, the attacks on you, the mountains you are climbing, the cuts, the bruises, the scars—God wastes nothing. Weather the weather, whether you want to or not.

AFFIRMATION

By the grace of God, I will never look like what I have gone through.

DAY 20

MORE THAN A CONQUEROR

> "No, in all these things we are more than conquerors through him who loved us." (Romans 8:37 – NIV).

Moments before the news of my dad's passing, I woke up with a song in my head, "More Than a Conqueror" by Rondell Positive. When I got the news, I immediately realized that this song was given to me as a token that whatever happened in this season, I am already a conqueror. Oh, and they did come: the sleepless nights, nightmares, thoughts of injustice, the feeling of being crushed by my reality, the idea that no one understands, thoughts of defeat; they all came. However, I found myself repeating these words *"I'm more than a conqueror."* This did not create a false sense that my father would return from death, but it shifted me to a lively hope that better days were ahead. It did not suppress how I felt, but it gave me reasons to want to go through it.

This gift of promise presented an alternative premise to dwell on instead of the hopelessness of death, and my task was to keep this alternative alive by reminding myself of it every time the thoughts of defeat came. The promise of God in times of death, disappointment, and despair is not one that is calling you to be a superhero, show up every time, and being great. Instead, He is calling you to make a move in the direction of hope every day amidst the feeling of defeat because, in all these things, you are more than a conqueror. Each of us gets a promise of hope in our deepest, darkest state of despair and devastation. Some lose it in the overwhelming sea of hopelessness and helplessness. For others, it is the glimmer of better days ahead. What is your promise, and how are you treating it? The promise of God empowers you to overcome, make use of it and guard it. Keep it away from the lies of the enemy and the piercing doubt your current reality brings.

AFFIRMATION

I hope in despair. I rise from defeat. I hold fast to the promise that says I can. I'm more than a conqueror.

DAY 21

FIND AN OUTLET

"When I kept silent, my bones wasted away through my groaning all day long." (Psalm 32:3 – NIV).

There is at least one person in your sphere who is willing to listen. They may not understand. They may not know what to say, but they will listen. Never underestimate the power of a listening ear. On one occasion, I had a nightmare. It felt real. I was sweating, panting, and gasping for breath with streams of tears flowing effortlessly down my face. I called Trudy, who came, listened, then prayed.

You do not have to talk until you are ready. You are under absolutely no obligation to because, the truth is, the nature of trauma sometimes steals your expressive abilities and forces you to bottle up your emotions. This is dangerous. Find an outlet that will help you. When talking was difficult, the ink in a pen became my tears, and my notepad the shoulders I cried on—I wrote.

What is your outlet? The Psalmist said his bones were wasted through his groaning all day long because he kept silent (see Psalm 32:3-5). Bones here represent support and structure. You being silent does nothing but invalidate your support system and shakes up your structure. Release that which burdens you and furnish those around you with how they can help. The way out starts with letting it out.

AFFIRMATION

The way out starts by letting it out.

DAY 22

THE DANCING SUGARCANE

"I remember the days of long ago; I meditate on all your works and consider what your hands have done. I spread out my hands to you; I thirst for you like a parched land." (Psalm 143:5-6 – NIV).

As a rural child, I take pride in how much I love sugarcane. Maybe this love came out of an experience worth cherishing. My home is situated on top of a slope, and it is the first house off the main road, about five meters in. I could stand at my fence and see about fifty meters out on the main road just before it makes a turn into a corner. This was my lookout point every evening for my dad as he made his way home from the farm. I would look to see if he had that one sugarcane dancing on his shoulder as he made his way home, and I would then run to meet him, smiling from ear to ear. At this point, I was the happiest girl alive.

Recanting these experiences caused a surge of unbridled joy that thrust me into a state of gratitude. I found that because these were good experiences, I had a reason to smile in memory of him. I found a good place to dwell, and this gave me a reason to smile amidst the adversity. A smile does not only transfigure your face, but it also transforms your outlook. Once your mind is in a place to conceive a positive thought, you are in a position to accept your reality, and acceptance strategically prepares you to move along. When you look back with gratitude, you can then look ahead with hope, and live worthwhile in this present moment.

AFFIRMATION

I dwell in peace. I choose to smile. I move; I move along.

DAY 23

SLOW DOWN BUT NEVER STOP LIVING

"Come to me, all you who are weary and burdened, and I will give you rest." (Matthew 11:28 – NIV).

Death is an unexpected turn on this journey of life. My dad died in a motor vehicle accident the same night I went back to school in January 2018. I had registered to do five modules, coupled with being a student-athlete and student-leader. I took a decision that slowed down my tenure at Utech Jamaica by a year, but it was worth it. I dropped three of the modules I was scheduled to sit. This gave me adequate breathing space to process the ordeal while still making small strides toward my goals.

Slowing down might look different for you. It could be taking a few days from work, temporarily relinquishing your responsibilities or even changing your environment. Slow down but never stop living.

Here is a hard truth; life continues. While you are dealing with and processing death, keep this at the back of your mind and make decisions surrounding that. Give yourself an opportunity to bounce back instead of sacrificing your hope to continue. Slowing down helps you to assess, adjust, decide, and execute. When you slow down, you can honor God's invitation to come away and find rest.

AFFIRMATION

I'm striding slowly, but I'm striding still. There is an assured rest for me.

DAY 24

THE EAGLE'S PLIGHT: GRACE YOUR PACE

"but those who hope in the LORD will renew their strength. They will soar on wings like eagles; they will run and not grow weary, they will walk and not be faint." (Isaiah 40:31 – NIV).

The eagle is known as the most majestic bird, and it is admired for its tenacity and resilience. The story of the eagle is laced with inspiration and lessons to last a lifetime. However, its journey through the cleft when it must weather the weather of despair is often not looked at. Its time in the cleft comes about when its enemy, the crow, ruffles its feathers. This raffling causes its feathers to make noise, and this will drive away its prey, which means after a while, the eagle will be starving. To remove these raffled feathers, the eagle goes through a gruesome and bloody season. In this season, the old feathers are removed, new ones grow, and the eagle stays in the cleft of the rock during this time.

Death is one experience that will ruffle your feathers, and if you don't cleft and cleft well, your vulnerabilities will be exposed to the enemy who is waiting to take you out. The eagle waits in the cleft. It receives new growth in the cleft. It is fed and supported in the cleft. Its time in the cleft demonstrates patience and showing the power in waiting.

As you navigate life with these new and despairing developments, give yourself grace as you feel the emotions, battle the internal battles, endure the severance from what you knew to be normal, and strategize for the way forward. In due time, your strength will come. What has ruffled your feathers? Nothing the Lord has you go through is to your detriment. The cleft is a lonely place and can be viewed as isolation and rejection, but you can turn that into a place of separation for preparation and restoration. Your strength will come, and you will be reaching new heights.

AFFIRMATION

I am made better for going through the cleft.

DAY 25

THE BROOK IS DRIED

"Sometime later the brook dried up because there had been no rain in the land." (1 Kings 17:7 – NIV).

Sometimes we feel flagged out and worn, but it is all a part of the process. What is beautiful is that even in this state, we still extend ourselves to others. It is indeed beautiful. In fact, it is great, but is it wise? Know when your environment is no longer serving you, and be bold enough to detach from it. If your environment is not feeding you to nourishment, it is sucking you dry to your detriment. If you are not growing there, you are dying there.

The journey of life has unexpected turns that thrust you off balance and shake up your reality. What do you do then? Give up? God forbids! Start looking out by assessing your environment. Plant biology tells you that growth takes place where the soil is not contaminated, a sufficient supply of water is present, and sunlight is readily accessible. In our lives, these same three categories of people make up our environment. They are either helping to clear our clutter or contaminating us, watering us, draining us, exposing us to transformational possibilities, or suffocating our potential.

Elijah was being fed at the brook, but the brook was dried up because something had changed in the environment. When that happens, it is time to change your position. Too many of us are satisfied with a short-lived belly full—sacrificing our purpose to be accommodating. The brook is dry; get up and go!

AFFIRMATION

I will cut off whatever or whoever doesn't serve me well.

POEM: 'THOU I WALK!'

Valleys low, mountains high
He has not called you to die here
Seek ye the Lord,
You'll find strength when the time gets hard
Though seeking the Lord is a relationship that perpetuates beyond break up, persevere through breakouts and promulgate peace.

Peace, peace like a stream of fresh water fed to the parched
Crashing like thunder against the rocks that should have stoned me to death
Composing an orchestra of assurance
Choreographing a piece that speaks to every move
Is necessary for even those who thrust to you and you relinquished control.
That's how the valleys got really low!

So low, I could hardly feel my face
Numb by the ambiance this path aired
I wondered for days where the grace to see this to the end was.
Then, like lightning running breathlessly from the eastern skies, my commitment flashed before my eyes.
Oh, commitments!
Commitment is not for the smooth patches

It is for the days when life questions your resolve to push and persevere
When you are called to stand in the face of doubt and adversity
Discomfort with the threat of a shattered destiny.

I press toward the mark;
The valley is not where it ends
I will not end where I start.
Mountains high, I'm coming to the top
Make note, the beginning of the next stair is the point where I stopped.
Each experience in the valley is a platform from which to launch
That's how God transforms into good what was meant to bring me harm
Valleys low, but mountains high
Yet still I rise to weather the weather, whether I want to or not.

A CALL TO PRAY:

DO NOT COUNT ME OUT

To the God who gives power, love and a sound mind in the stead of fear I pray. Here on this job, I stepped out knowing that the chances of death, injury and loss is not virtually nil due to the high risk associated with my service. A commitment to service means putting my life on the line and this mantles me with a crippling fear that wants me to tap out. I see and hear of colleagues dying every day (both young and old) at the hand of the miscreants of society. I see the fear in the eyes of my families every time I have to leave home. I feel the weight of under-compensation and the burden and strain it places on us. The injustices in the system are exhausting!

I hear of colleagues succumbing to suicidal thoughts because fear has gripped them with a strangling hold. I don't count myself better that them but for the fact that I am alive, I'm here, I get to see the glee and unbridled joy on the faces of my family when I return home, I thank You and it is against that background that I pray. Continue to undergird us as we weather the weather whether we want to or not. We don't always understand why we lose the one we lose so I pray for the grace to see and know that You waste nothing and we are more than conquerors. I thank You that You are the most trusted outlet and confidant.

Help us to accept that life will slow us down but grant us grace to R.U.N – return to who and whose we are, undergird ourselves with Your truth and to never give up even if it's the easier way out. I declare that the losses we face will not weaken us to ruins but will prepare us for the return of Christ, in Jesus' name. Amen.

CHAPTER 4

THE COMMANDER'S VOICE

In training, there is the concept of morning discipline that was classified into physical training and drill. Drill was my favourite because it presented something new and challenged me to do something I had never done before. When I became the commander of my squad, my passion for the discipline increased, and I had a different perspective. I believed if all my squad mates were exposed to giving commands, the squad would have a great chance of being on top. However, the reality is, that was never feasible.

Being a commander expanded my horizon on how God views us and how we respond. God sees us as perfect, but we respond with imperfections. Notwithstanding, our reactions do not taint God's view of us.

On one evening of training, I gave a command, and a member of the squad did the opposite. At this point, one member was looking directly into the face of another while the rest of the squad was aligned as commanded. If you have ever been in this position, you will know that this is a very uncomfortable place to be in. So it is with us in life. We make mistakes, they put us in uncomfortable positions, and we become flustered, ashamed, and embarrassed. In this moment, the commander sees this it is his/her job to give another command to get everyone in alignment. This is really beautiful because I have come to learn that that is how God operates. From this experience, I discovered a few things about God:

- He commands us based on the intended outcome He has and not based on where we want to go.
- God does not leave us to the mercy of our mistakes.
- He expects us to give grace to each other.

As a commander, you will learn that there are two phases to a command: the phase of caution and the phase of execution. The phase of caution tells you the specific task to be done, and the phase of execution is when to carry out the task.

If we look at the command for an "about turn," the aim of such a command is to get the squad to face the front of the parade. The commander will say, "The squad will advance" and this is the caution. When the commander says "about turn," this is when you are required to move. If you miss this time pedal, you miss the point.

God instructs us to move when the time comes for us to move. Between God's instruction and your execution, there is preparation that is often overlooked. Too many people are moving ill-equipped and unprepared. If God calls you, He will equip you. When does this happen? Between Him calling and you moving. If God sends you, He prepares you. When does this happen? Between Him sending and you going. Let's consider the story of David. He was anointed king years before he ascended to the thrown, and between those times, he was being prepared for his reign.

The commander's voice is as instructive as it is cautionary, and it takes hours of rehearsal to build a chemistry between the squad and commander. God cannot influence our lives if we fail to spend time with Him. If we must follow the commander, we must know the commander. His commands are clear; they offer guidance, challenge our limitations and restore us to our respective places.

The commander's voice uses drill commands to indicate his intentions, and close attention must be paid to when he says it and how he says it. This is synonymous with God's voice, and you will see this in this chapter. Here, also, the mechanism of standing still is underscored, the value of making a needed "about turn" is emphasized, and the importance of being ready to move when the command is given is expressed. It also highlights what tools we have in our arsenal to survive and thrive.

DAY 26

WHERE HE LEADS

"I will instruct you and teach you in the way you should go; I will counsel you with my loving eye on you." (Psalm 32:8 – NIV).

The idea of providence tells us that God has an expected end for all of us. This is also a promise He intends to fulfil in our lives. As a result, His commands are to guide us along a path to that promised, expected end. God says, **"For I know the plans I have for you," declares the Lord, "plans to prosper you and not to harm you, plans to give you hope and a future." (Jeremiah 29:11 - NIV).** When the commander is tasked to perform a march pass, for example, he knows where he wants the parade to go at a given time, and he will give the requisite instructions to get you there. He is also looking ahead to ensure there is no obstruction, and if there is, he figures out how he will have you navigate around it. Therefore, your struggles do not surprise God. If God has a preview of your life, why would you not trust Him to lead you?

There are many answers in heaven to prayers that no one bothered to pray. You have one job; to consult the Commander before moving. Failure to trust God's guidance comes from not knowing what will happen next, and this brings about uncertainties. In times of uncertainty, we must trust the only one who is certain. In leading you, God knows what you need, when you need it, and what proportions you need, and He will stop at nothing until you get it.

As I stood to command my squad on the day of a drill completion, there was an aspect that I had to call a "mark time." This is rigorous and demands a lot of physical strength. I noticed one of my squad mates who was not as fit as the others losing it; running out of breath. If I failed to respond to observation, I would destroy the integrity of the drill because she was going to fall. God doesn't overlook your need, and it doesn't matter how minute they seem. Once He sees His child in need, He runs toward him. God leads but also comes down to hold your hand when it is hard. God gives you a moment to breathe, so just breathe!

AFFIRMATION

My future is secured. Oh, for grace to trust God as my Commander and follow Him as my leader.

DAY 27

THE WRONG RIGHT TURN

"Then David comforted his wife Bathsheba, and he went to her and made love to her. She gave birth to a son, and they named him Solomon. The Lord loved him; and because the Lord loved him, he sent word through Nathan the prophet to name him Jedidiah." (2 Samuel 12:24-25 – NIV).

God will not condone our mistakes, but He certainly won't kill us for making them. However, He expects us to be prudent and learn from them. David lost the first child he had with Bathsheba because he messed up badly. He committed adultery. He lied and murdered one of his foot soldiers. David was in battle for his entire reign, and one of his biggest enemies was raised in his household because of this poor decision.

To make a mistake is human, and you will pay for it, but God does not condemn you. He gives you a second chance. Out of the union between David and Bathsheba bore a son who was suitable to take over the reign of David when the time was right. Good can come out of a bad situation, and there are reasons for you not to give up. Don't give up on you, and don't give up on God's grace to restore you. God's commands do not force us because, if it were so, there would not be room for mistakes. Instead, they empower us to move in a certain direction. When empowerment takes root, action grows. Growth builds confidence, and confidence is what stands between you and endless possibilities. In honor of my mistakes, I am better for having made them because I have learned from them, and I found a new level of grace to pursue a better me.

AFFIRMATION

I am not defined by my mistakes. I am a perfect picture painted by broken pieces. I am saved by grace, and that is where peace is.

DAY 28

STAND STILL

"Bear with each other and forgive one another if any of you has a grievance against someone. Forgive as the Lord forgave you." (Colossians 3:13 – NIV).

We do not give each other grace. We find it hard to forgive. We do not sympathize with each other as we should and, until someone dies, we never try to acknowledge their humanity. Why? When I gave the command and my squad mate made the wrong turn, the rest of the squad stood still. They knew one person blundered, but they stood still. When they stood still, they were giving the commander an opportunity to right the wrong. It also indicated that they accepted this blunder as a mistake and one they were also prone to make.

If the squad had gone into an uproar at the blunder, it would have eaten at the confidence of the one who erred, creating no room to make it right. Standing still means giving grace. This is hard because you are really hurt, but you can do it. This is hard to do because we are in an age that celebrates cutting people off as they err. This age tells you that love ends when you have done me wrong, and it doesn't endure anything. That is one of the biggest lies we have been accepting as normal. We must give each other the leverage to bounce back. How many times would you want to be forgiven? I suspect as many times as you err, and you should be. Now, extend the same grace to someone else.

AFFIRMATION

Grace is not selfish because we all need it at some point.

DAY 29

GENERAL SALUTE, PRESENT ARMS

"The LORD turned to him and said, "Go in the strength you have and save Israel out of Midian's hand. Am I not sending you?" (Judges 6:14 – NIV).

As we advanced in training, we were given 303 rifles to keep and care for, and these were the same ones we did rifle drill exercises with both in rehearsal and on the day of the competition. These rifles went through a whole, but when it was time to present arms, those rifles were required to be flying in the air in regulation time. Some were broken, some were falling apart, and others were so damaged they had to be replaced. There is a truth about God that this exercise amplified. It may not blow your mind, but it will help you understand that He can use you if you just come as you are. God uses what you have left, not what you had or wish you had.

"Present arms" is a command of execution given in the highest compliment paid in our organization—a general salute—and it requires us to come with the tattered arms that you have. Your brokenness will honor God! God will not refuse you because life has bruised you. God will not reject you because the process has broken you. God will not ignore the sincere cry of those low in spirit. He is close to the brokenhearted. He strengthens the hands of the weak. God told Gideon to go in his strength (see Judges 6:14). What strength? Note that Gideon was honest with God about how he felt about himself. Maybe that was where his strength was—in his willingness to accept his weakness and broken state. Amidst this reality, God called out the strength in him. Regardless of how you feel about yourself, God sees strength; He sees a fighter, He sees a victor; He sees courage in you. He knows that with Him, you can push the limits.

AFFIRMATION

I don't feel like it, but life has prepared me to be strong, and God has called me to be brave. I was born a fighter, and fight I will. The great grows from brokenness, and I am nothing less.

DAY 30

FALL OUT

"Come to me, all you who are weary and burdened, and I will give you rest." (Matthew 11:28 – NIV).

After a long session of rigorous drilling, everyone's greatest desire is to hear the command "Fall Out." Upon this command, the parade makes a right turn and takes five marching paces. Thereafter, they are free to go take a break, rehydrate, rest, replenish their strength, and catch their breath. So it is with this life after a long season of battling ailments, fighting internal battles, being stretched by life's demands, making mistakes and paying for them, being hurt, suffering, bruised; God gently calls you to come away and rest.

Retreating is an important part of climbing. By the nature of climbing, you get tired and worn out, so make time to take a break. Schedule a break on your calendar and be ruthless about it. Show me a man who doesn't rest, and I can tell he is digging his own grave with his hands.

The story of Samson records an occasion when he used a donkey's jawbone to defeat the Philistine army and, shortly after their demise, Samson got weary and thirsty. He cried out to God, *"I did such a great job. Will You cause me to die of thirst?"* God opened a brook and replenished him. God responds to our honesty and despises our pretense. You cannot be effective when you are fatigued, flagged, and worn. You have been fighting on your own. God's invitation is simple: *"Come unto Me, and I'll give you rest!" (see Matthew 28:11).*

AFFIRMATION

Falling out doesn't mean I have fallen. It's a phase where the worn is replenished, the weak is strengthened, the broken gets to heal, and tired finds rest. I fall out as often as I need to.

POEM: 'GEORGE'

Clear vision but broken sight
   Strong faith but shattered might;
   It was by your Spirit anyways
Anyways, I a gwaan look fi si wah gwaan
There are more than a million reasons to call it George
Yet again, I've found one reason to call you LORD
You just never fail
Weh George a guh?"

George is giving up
George is settling for less
George is whispering "You're the worst, even at your best."
George is saying "Forget the full-term process,
Birthing is too painful, and it doesn't make sense."
George says "Your sacrifice will not be honoured;
your loss lost its recompense."
George is shouting, "You can no longer fight.
You are weak, and you are frail."

How many times has George told you how miserably you have failed?
How many times have your "georgeous" thoughts incarcerated you with no plans to sanction your bail?

Today is prison break, and to the gallows George was led.
We hung that crippling voice that has been parading in your head
I have waited for this moment, finally, today, George is dead.

About turn!
I turn about the axis of my mistakes, and heard when your voice said still come
It's human to believe George, but I command you to run
There were more than a million reasons to call it George
But I have found just enough reason to call you Lord
Your voice makes a difference.

A CALL TO PRAY:

FIGHT FOR ME

Commander of the army of Israel, fight for me. I have long stopped listening for the voice of the commander because the cheers of excitement and shouts of celebration coupled with the noise of the naysayers have drown out the commands and instructions being given. I have been out of step and alignment, and I have made some wrong right turns.

So today, I call my mind back into focus so I can hear You once again. Give me grace to return to the drill square of Your Word so that I can parade Your truth in every move I make. Give me the wisdom to listen to the precaution, the know-how to execute every move in the right timing and then stand still and see You at work in my life, my family, my posts, station, section or department, my community and the nation at large. May it be, before I fall out, that I'll go where You lead, Commander, and that as in the true meaning of a General Salute, my works will bring glory to Your name.

Before I fall out, may I make every wrong turn right; before I fall out, may I salute You as the general of my life. Before I fall out, grant me the grace to see that You never stopped fighting for me, in Jesus' name. Amen.

CHAPTER 5

SLOW MARCH

If your chase is not leaving a trace, you are not running your race. Quit the haste time to find your pace and leave a trace. Haste makes waste!

On the heels of 2020, I received this thought of inspiration that added some perspective to my life. I believe it will be helpful to share here. The concept of slow march comes from drilling, and this I learned when I was in training. Apart from the fact that slow marching is beautiful to watch and graceful to execute, there are, of course, some underlying truths that I could not ignore because, for starters, it allows me to appreciate the exercise and make learning it easier. They have great inspirational value and wisdom and can relate to our day-to-day lives. These truths are:

- Slow march develops balance and good carriage.
- It requires strategically putting one foot after the other.
- It requires you to put your foot down when necessary.

BALANCE AND GOOD CARRIAGE

The way forward cannot be achieved without balance. Balance is not the idea that there must be equal weights at both ends, neither is it the measure of the amount of mass a thing carries. Rather it is a principle of life. Balance is appreciating the yen and yang of life. It is the willingness to give as much as you take. Balance is the idea that when I make a move, others fall into place as opposed to being scattered and disarrayed. This outlines that moving forward requires alignment with your own purpose. Therefore, you will find that the principle of balance urges you not to compare your race with that of another because you are uniquely equipped with what you need for your journey. Your race requires your skills and idiosyncrasies, and the moment you begin to pry at that with the tool of comparison, you begin to cripple your creative abilities, thus, throwing your system off balance.

Being a good carriage speaks to camaraderie, the ability to move along in cohesion. If you are not ready to work as a group, you are not ready for life. This highlights the importance of partnering as a means to bring to life the potential of each member. Until we learn to work together, we will remain in the cycle of failure. Selfishness is a predominant theme that we face as a people. This unbalances the system.

Put one foot after the other. Mom taught me this saying, "If you run too quickly, you'll run twice." I see where in executing a slow march, you must strategically put one foot before the other. What is this teaching us? Strategize, then execute. Be patient and consistent in your efforts and you will see results.

Here is a mistake we make: we sow today and want to reap tomorrow, and when the inevitable happens, we lose hope. Success is the sum total of the decisions we make over time. While growing up with the boys back home, I learned u calabans—a mechanism they used when bird hunting. They set it with the right bait and leave it over a period of time. This principle is still in effect today. Society will tell you there are ways around this, and indeed there are, but they all lead you back to square one. You choose to put one foot after the other strategically.

Put your foot down when it's necessary. We have been called an invertebrate generation—lacking firm principles on which we stand. In slow march, the troop is required to drive their feet firmly to the ground when coming to a halt. In life, we are called to put our foot down when our moral principles and values are being violated, when our energy is being drained without replenishment, and when our stance is being questioned. There is a sacrifice that comes with this, one that many are not willing to make.

The people who will leave a trace on this earth are those who stand for something and have the ability to decipher the subtle breaches, and there are many.

In this chapter, the devotionals are geared toward bringing clarity to your own race being run strategically, patiently, and consistently. Comparison cripples creativity; selfishness obliterates impact; impatience thwarts flow, and haste interrupts balance.

DAY 31

COMPARISON IS A THIEF

"We do not dare to classify or compare ourselves with some who commend themselves. When they measure themselves by themselves and compare themselves with themselves, they are not wise." (2 Corinthians 10:12 – NIV).

Each person must understand his own abilities to bring balance to a team. Your strengths and weaknesses are what makes you unique, and they are what makes you fit in where you do belong. I will never understand why everyone wants to be so much alike. Comparison cripples your creative ability, thereby limiting the scope of your reach. God says those who compare themselves are without understanding (see 2 Corinthians 10:12). This is the understanding: it is one Spirit—the Spirit of God—who enables and empowers each individual. Let us not confuse admiration with comparison. There are those who you will look up to, but when you try to become like them, you begin living a lie. Where there is a lie, there is no peace of mind, there is a lack of contentment, there arises the inferiority complex, and low self-esteem persists.

Be different and do differently; that is Holy Ghost inspired creativity that comparison wants to destroy. Embrace your limitations; you are human. Never forget that God does not use what you wish you have.

AFFIRMATION

I have within me what it takes to live a balanced life, and comparison suffocates my creativity. I am me. I am different, and my difference is needed.

DAY 32

YOUR LANE, YOUR SKILLS, YOUR BLESSINGS

"For he ruled over all the kingdoms west of the Euphrates River, from Tiphsah to Gaza, and had peace on all sides." (1 Kings 4:24 – NIV).

I always admire the relationship between Solomon and David. Though not much is spoken of, there is more to be desired from this story, from the theme of beauty painted from imperfections and mistakes to how relentless the love of God is. The most beautiful aspect of this story is when both are viewed separately. David was the warrior king, and Solomon was the king who had peace at his borders. David's talent got him a seat at the table of his destiny. Solomon's wisdom got him a place in the heart of the people he served. David's might gave him dominance, and Solomon's peace attracted from afar off. Two kings, two lanes, different skill sets, both with blessings beyond measure.

Solomon knew he would have to run his race, and upon assuming his position on the throne, he got rid of everything and everyone that would challenge the deployment of his skills and, thus, thwart his blessings (see 1 Kings 2:23-46). Solomon's reign was laced with peace. What if he wanted to prove that he was as mighty as David? He would have engaged in battles that were not even battles to begin with. There is a grace that comes with staying in your lane. Apply your skills and the inevitable blessings can be overstated. When we step out of our lanes, we step into a war we are not equipped for, and as a result, we become low on energy, frustrated with the journey, and angry at life. Stay in your lane. That is where the peace you have been searching for is.

AFFIRMATION

My lane requires all the energy I possess. I refuse to fight any unnecessary battles, and my blessings will not be thwarted.

DAY 33

ONE HAND WASHES THE OTHER

"**For as the body is one, and hath many members, and all the members of that one body, being many, are one body: so also is Christ.**" (1 Corinthians 12:12 – KJV).

Understanding one's uniqueness and abilities is the first step to fighting selfishness, hence, the value placed on learning about one's self. There is, however, this truth: the world does not revolve around you alone. The beauty of the slow march cannot be seen when one person is doing it, and this teaches us that in this life, everyone with the right efforts placed in the right places can win. We must actively and intentionally dismiss the thought that success is only for a few; it is selfish and it is crippling, and because this is the prevailing idea among our people, there is hardly any unity.

Think about the head fighting against the feet that have the responsibility to move it from point to point. Imagine the heart saying it won't send any blood to the eyes because they get to see everything. How ridiculous! It is indeed ridiculous, but it is not farfetched. Christ dismissed the idea of selfishness, yet it is evident among our people: members fighting members or members not sharing resources with another because it might just make them look good. The truth is, in a system, if the feet move, so does the head, and until we view us being links in one chain, we remain stuck in unhealthy and failing cycles. Your actions, or the lack thereof, affect me as much as mine affects you. We do not exist in a vacuum, isolated from each other. The principle that one hand washes the other is still true. When you win, I win. When I win, you win. When you pull the rug from under your colleague, you inadvertently pull the rug from under you. Do I need to be selfish? No, we are one body, each part having its specific responsibilities. There is no place for selfishness in advancement because one man's strength covers the other one's weakness.

AFFIRMATION

I walk away from my selfish tendencies for the greater good of my team.

DAY 34

HOW MUCH CAN YOU BEAR?

"And no one pours new wine into old wineskins. Otherwise, the wine will burst the skins, and both the wine and the wineskins will be ruined. No, they pour new wine into new wineskins." (Mark 2:22 – NIV).

It never occurred to me that the popular saying "God nah give you more than you can bear" could have a different and, by extension, a deeper meaning than what we are used to. We are used to this expression relating to our ability to go through and overcome challenges, but never to see it relative to our purpose.

Let's look at the word "bear" as used in the expression; it means to carry. This now opens up the conversation and causes us to think deeper. If something must be carried, there must be a carriage. The ability of the carriage to carry relies heavily on the structure and whether it is intact or broken. If you see yourself as a carriage, you must think about your ability to carry because if the structural integrity of your carriage is compromised, you cannot carry much or anything for that matter. Do you feel like you have been in one place too long, not experiencing more, not doing more, not being more? Check your carriage; see if there exists the possibility of leakage because God does not waste anything. He gives what is needed when it is needed and in the appropriate proportion. He will not pour into you if you are going to slow leak. Check your carriage. How much can you truly handle? When wine is poured into an old wine skin, two things happen:

1. The wineskin breaks.
2. The wine is wasted.

Can you handle what you have been praying for? Are you even stewarding what you already have? Think on these things.

Now, every carriage has a capacity, and it is pointless to put a square in a circle. The beauty about us is that our carriage can stretch; it is flexible. Therefore, in order to carry/bear more than we are used to, we must engage in capacity building: expand your horizon, shift your mindset, thrust yourself to new experiences, and subject yourself to be taught, coached and mentored. Increase your ability to carry. You won't get more than you can bear; don't be fooled!

AFFIRMATION

I possess the ability to do and be more; my capacity can expand beyond my limitations.

DAY 35

MY ENERGY GOES BEFORE ME

"And Jesus, immediately knowing in himself that virtue had gone out of him, turned him about in the press, and said, Who touched my clothes?" (Mark 5:30 – KJV).

Another life principle coming from slow marching is assessing your energy. Unlike the quick march, the slow march has a lower tempo, requires less energy, and usually covers larger distances. Have you ever wondered why you can't get a certain degree of energy and support from your team? Check your energy. You will radiate what is inside of you.

The energy you give off creates an aura around you, and this aura is like a signboard; it either reads "You're welcome" or "Get lost." People can read this energy, and it extensively influences your interaction with them. Bad energy is repulsive because it gives off a stench and not an aroma. When the energy is repulsive, there is unproductivity and bare minimum performance because no one genuinely cares about you. They know that care will not be reciprocated. It is as important to balance energy as it is to balance the books. People knew that being in the presence of Jesus would bring life to their dead situations. What does your presence bring? Does it bring hope or condemnation; does it bring wisdom or folly; does it bring peace or war? Does it bring hate or love? Does it provide inclusion?

Another aspect of assessing your energy is being able to decipher what deserves your time and what doesn't. In the same story, there were many pulling at Jesus wanting His attention, but He held His composure and maintained His based on what was priority: the needy. In taking a page from Jesus' book, we ought to place our energy where it is needed. Remember, swine have no use for pearls except to make a mess of them. Choose wisely where you exert your energy.

AFFIRMATION

I will ensure that when energy proceeds from me, it brings life, restores hope, and lightens the atmosphere. My energy precedes me!

DAY 36

A BALCONY VIEW

"So the people took victuals in their hand, and their trumpets: and he sent all the rest of Israel every man unto his tent, and retained those three hundred men: and the host of Midian was beneath him in the valley." (Judges 7:8 – KJV).

Team spirit, support, sacrifice, camaraderie, and growth are all characteristics of any group of people that is going somewhere. Those in your corner should influence you to push the limits while you do the same.

Upon returning from training, I visited my brother, Brucelee. His balcony gives you a view of what I call a mini forest. You could see trees and plants, hear the chirping of the birds harmonizing with sound and see a gentle stream flowing in the distance. As therapeutic as this ambiance was, I was distracted by the size of the trees I was looking at. They were all huge and tall trees. Among the trees were fruit trees like orange, lemon, ackee, and coconut, and these too were large and tall. I was taken aback because I had never seen an orange tree rubbing shoulders with a coconut tree. It is a concept in ecology that the environment in which a habitat is will influence the development of its organisms. These trees challenged each other to be above average and, as it is within this mini forest, so it is with us. We can measure how far we will go by the people we surround ourselves with; your circle. God demonstrated this principle when He filtered Gideon's army from thousands down to three hundred. Your circle does not have to be large; it only needs to have persons who will go as far as they can go to achieve the goal. Your circle should challenge you to be better and do better; be a better family person, be a better businessman, and make life-changing as opposed to life-threatening decisions. Your circle should be able to sow seeds of wisdom, freely use the rod of correction, brace and embrace and celebrate the mileage of everyone.

Here is another truth you ought to sow into your circle in accordance with your measure of strength. Your circle should feed your spirit and not drain your soul. An important aspect of Gideon's 300 is that they directed glory to God. This, my friend, ought to be your life's goal. Too often, we are inclined to believe that it is our own strength that is giving us success. I commend your efforts, your demonstration of strength, your consistency and discipline, but note very well that it is God who gives the increase.

AFFIRMATION

If my circle is growing, so am I. If my circle is lacking, so am I. I can measure how far I'm going by who I am going with, but I can also push those I'm with a little further than they would go without me.

DAY 37

IMPATIENCE THWARTS FLOW

"A little one shall become a thousand, and a small one a strong nation: I the Lord will hasten it in his time." (Isaiah 60:22 – KJV).

In a ceremonial event, a march is usually one of the purposes a parade serves, and the slow march initiates this process. As the parade advances around the drill square, you will observe the seamless, graceful flow as each person stays within the regulation time, each file after the other, stepping out when necessary and stopping short when it is needed. If one person moves just a beat above this pace, it throws off the grace and beauty of the march.

There are strategic points along the drill square that require different actions, for example, a left wheel or a left turn, and if one person goes out of line, it thrusts the parade into shambles. Wait for the correct timing because when the timing is right, everything falls into place as it should. As the intricacies of the slow march tire and wear out the squads, so does having to wait in life wear you to frustration. However, it is in waiting that you see

God taking your little efforts and turning them into big successes. In waiting, you learn to aim; in waiting, you receive alignment; in waiting, you learn consistency; in waiting, you master the art of strategically putting one foot behind the other as you press towards your goals; it is in waiting that you learn to ride the rhythm of life's most treacherous waves and create a beautiful and graceful flow. If you grow while you wait, your flow can never be threatened by impatience.

AFFIRMATION

The wait is where the work takes place. It is where I become grounded and prepared to stand balanced. The wait is worth it.

POEM: 'LET THE SCIENCE SPEAK'

Momentum does it
　Mass by velocity
　　Velocity being displacement over time
Displacement meaning your movement is not arbitrary
Intentional efforts placed in the right place within the appropriate time does it
Life and its pressures will thrust you to the fast line and if you can't keep up, just like that, you are tossed into thin air
How volatile
It's like you were never there.

Pressure breaks or makes you
Pressure being force applied over a surface area
Force, the weight you moved at a distance within a time frame
You are forced to make it now
And if you don't, you are to be blamed
Live like it's your last, they say
But if it's your last, most of your life is in the past, maybe
The pressure is getting worse, so let's talk about you first
Pressure only burst a pipe that wasn't meant to carry it
"He will not give you if you cannot bear it."

Do you see that life can thrust you into a temporary fix?
Take your time
Do you
Build you
That's the way to balance it.

Balance, rest, equilibrium
Take time to measure how far you have come
Distance is measured in meters, and time in seconds
You are measured in the effect of what you do and not your intentions
Distance is measured by a rule
Time by watch
You are measured by how many times you've failed to give and not by the times you had to stop
You have fought a good fight
You stuck to the notion
Action begets an equal but opposite reaction
A consistent momentum, even as the pressure rises
Speaks volume to the treasure that you have inside
Striding slowly but striding still!

A CALL TO PRAY:

PROTECT ME FROM BAD-MIND AND THE BAD-MINDED

The only pure God, You are immutable and infallible, but, me, I am tainted by sin and often times conflicted. I know I am not absolved from the frailty of the flesh. I cry for help! When I see the talents and gifts You have placed in others, the favour and accomplishments, the promotions and uncommon favour, I ponder in my heart these things and with my egotistic nature, my thoughts get corrupted and truth flee from me. I now know that it is easy to become bad-minded—why am I not the one being promoted, why is that one shining more than me, I know I can do that better, why did I not get that opportunity?

Over time, the root of bitterness that I have planted by harbouring these thoughts spring up in the tree of envy bearing fruits of lust, jealousy, covetousness and corruption. The leaves of un-fulfillment now provide shade for sabotage, self-centeredness, mischief, malice, ill-will and hypocrisy. But I read somewhere that a small axe can cut a big tree down so, I appeal to you.

Dear Jesus, let Your grace cut down the tree of lies that is in my life and let Your shed blood curse the bitter roots that are deeply entrenched in me. Then, I will be able to accept my uniqueness, appreciate my talents, develop my skills, walk in my own lane and count my blessings. I will rise above comparison and be empowered to collaborate and not compete. I will burn the garment of hate that is sewn by thread of envy and be adorned with the mind to celebrate and cheer others on. I will strengthen the hands of the weak, and put back the dislocated joints in place.

Indeed Your favour breaks protocols, cause what is for me is mine to share in the advancement of Your people and my colleagues. I pray that by Your grace, You will expand my borders, but teach me to be humble. Protect me from bad-mind and the bad-minded, in Jesus' name. Amen.

CHAPTER 6

LONG ROUTE: WHEN PROMISE MEETS PREPARATION

Proper preparation prevents poor performance. In my earlier years, one of our chores was to fetch water from the community tank, which is about one and a half miles down a slope. The path was rocky and sometimes very slippery. If you thought getting there was hard, wait until you had to come up with the weight of the water in your hand or on your head. On one specific occasion, I was ascending the hill with a bucket of water on my head when I missed my step and the weight of the bucket twisted my neck. In that moment, I said to myself *"The things we have to do to stay well and keep going."* Nevertheless, that crooked path taught me to strategize and be resilient in execution.

Thereafter, I started identifying makers along the trail, and these would be the points where I would stop on my way up to take a break and re-gather myself. The more I did this, the easier the trip to the community tank became and, in this crooked situation, I discovered a life hack. When you act without planning, you are dwelling on chances, and there is no true hope of success. When you dwell on chance, you are just hoping it will happen; however, when you plan and then act, your actions are based on possibilities, giving you a better chance at navigating the challenges that will come. With this strategic intentionality, you will find beauty and blessings where opportunity meets preparation.

A long route is an unwanted break in transmission that sends you back to the preparation grounds because you were clearly not ready. The training felt like a punishment for mistakes made, and indeed it was because the instructors only sent you on this unenticing run when you messed up the drill. It took you through a rocky area with low-hanging thorns competing with the wind for your face. So, with your back bent, your hand as a shield, and your feet wobbling through the rocks, you bolt through phase one of the route.

On phase two, you come upon a high patch of grass, usually wet and cold and called the river, and indeed it is an oasis for your battered feet. Then on entering phase three, you pass the dumpster that takes your breath away. You are barely keeping up as you make it over that wall and down through the crooked stream to enter phase four: the home run. On this beautifully pave stretch, your legs are as heavy as death, and you get a chance to analyze your life. Do you want to do this again? Of course not, but you won't stop until you get it right.

In life, this long route is synonymous with the course of preparation and is very similar to the crooked path I had to travel to fetch water. It is rough. It gets stinky with the stench of your past that is hellbent on condemning you. Can you learn anything from this? Does this even make sense? You won't see that it does until the end where opportunities meet preparation and your mind is ready to show up and be great.

The course of preparation unlocks your potential, builds resilience, exposes your weakness, and gives you areas to work on. It shows you who can go to the next level with you.

On the course one morning, one of my squaddies had a challenge getting over the wall, and another picked her up on his back and carried her. That is someone you need at the next level with you; someone who will tune out the noise and help you.

Preparation helps you appreciate the rain for all it comes with. Preparation is the pain that births success. There are those persons who rose quickly because hype and links inflated them, but only the man who has the support of preparation and the substance from having gone through the process will last.

The long route is brutally pivotal! We have a responsibility to ensure that we are unlocking these character strengths daily and infusing this positive energy into our menus.

To help, here are seven days' worth of nuggets.

DAY 38

THIS CONFIDENCE

"being confident of this, that he who began a good work in you will carry it on to completion until the day of Christ Jesus." (Philippians 1:6 - NIV).

Have you ever stopped to notice that the people who are presumed to be confident have already gone through a lot in life? They have been on the course of preparation and, as a result, when they do stand, they know who and what is behind them.

Who is behind them? One of the hidden treasures intentionally embedded on the course of preparation is you finding grace to help in a time of need. This grace is supplied by God. Think about it for a moment; if it were not for the grace of God, would you have come out alive?

Your efforts are commendable. They show that you have faith, but it is God's grace that has sustained you. With this knowledge, you don't waver in your thoughts or stutter in your speech. You show up and deliver because the God who started and brought you this far can take you to completion. This confidence that makes us illuminate in everything we do has God all over it. This confidence with which we seamlessly pursue our purpose has God all over it. This confidence that we leave our homes with, knowing we will return, has God all over it. This confidence is built on the back of a God who cannot fail.

What is behind them? The support and substance of the process stand like a fortress behind those who obliged preparation, which amounts to the confidence, focus, and longevity they exude. You cannot forsake the phases of the course of preparation and think it will be well with you; it will not be.

AFFIRMATION

With the assurance that God is with me and the support of preparation behind me, I'm confident that amidst adversities that cause others to break, I am breaking records.

DAY 39

LET IT RAIN!

"There is a time for everything, and a season for every activity under the heavens: a time to be born and a time to die, a time to plant and a time to uproot." (Ecclesiastes 3:1-2 - NIV).

When it rains, let it rain. Do not focus on the rain. Consider the seeds you have sown. The rain does two things for seeds:

1. Makes them easier to be removed from the soil.
2. Prepares the soil for increase.

The rain represents a season in our lives when we do not necessarily have control over what is happening, but you are being impacted. Nobody likes this phase! First things first; you cannot will the rain away. There is nothing you can do to stop it. You just have to ride it out. It is how you ride it out that matters. The rain exposes you to things dry weather will not show you. It reveals areas of compromise that the dry weather CANNOT.

We all have planted some seeds in our speech, actions, and deeds. The beauty about seeds is that they become trees, but these can get ugly if the seeds are not sown from inner beauty. When seeds become trees, they are harder to get rid of; therefore, the rain comes to give you a chance to remove unwanted seeds from the soil. Seeds of backbite and hypocrisy produce the trees of mistrust. The seeds of laziness and nonchalance produce the tree of lack. Seeds sown in anger are still seeds whether you meant them or not, and they produce the tree of hurt. Let it rain. Allow the rain to wash away seeds that it can and, if it cannot, then it prepares the soil for you to remove them. We therefore need to stand up and face the blunt of the rain just to ensure some seeds don't grow. The rain empowers you to right wrongs only you can.

While you do that, there are also seeds that the rain prepares to grow and thus prepares you for increase. Your seeds will grow. Do you want them to?

AFFIRMATION

Today I remove every seed sown against the hope and future God has for me.

DAY 40

YOU'RE ABOVE YOUR PAST: MAKE IT COUNT

"Therefore, there is now no condemnation for those who are in Christ Jesus." (Romans 8:1 – NIV).

The past and its baggage are dissolved in the blood of Jesus, and the only way you can view it is as a token of the process and not as a big bad bully. You can't hate your past. It made you who you are today. There are people with an unhealthy obsession with the past and their past life that affects their current perspective on life, but the wise learn from the past and prepare in such a way as to prevent its reoccurrence.

A life of sin made you a child of the king today. A life of drugs, guns, prostitution, hypocrisy, and corruption gave you a voice of authority to those who are now so plagued. A life of a lie made you want to pursue truth today. A season of depression made you want to foster a positive mind, even in the darkest times, because you are not going back to that deep slimy pit. Yes, your past tragedies have equipped you with the strategies to make the future worth living.

Do not hate the route life took you through to find your purpose, whether it is the path you took or the path you were given. The purposes of God cannot be thwarted, so we are made the better for it.

If you find yourself going through it now, hating the process will not take you through any faster. In everything, always make the best of everything. Be an opportunist! Stop, assess where you are at, measure how far you are from your goal, and live to get to it. Your past created a path for you to have a great home run. Your job is to never return to that path as a victim but as a victor. Your path might have made you a victim, but it is your choice to live in victimhood. Your job is to lead someone else off that path. Your job is to live now like you deserve to because you deserve to.

As a child, I used to dread going home on Mondays because we had to go to somebody's farm to carry cane, bananas, plantain, and other produce for Miss Joy to take to market. Now, do I hate the people for the fact that we carried their load and still the larger percentage of the money went to them? Nah. The process was unfair, yes, but that was mom's way of ensuring we were cared for and we didn't end up with the same vulnerabilities.

You are empowered to live above your past. You are empowered to live above condemnation by suffering firsthand from it. If Christ does not condemn you, let no one else condemn you, NOT EVEN YOU!

AFFIRMATION

I am empowered to live above my past. I made it out alive. I won this time!

DAY 41

SHAKE AND DWEET

"The Sovereign Lord is my strength; he makes my feet like the feet of a deer, he enables me to tread on the heights." (Habakkuk 3:19 - NIV).

You, with God, is a majority! All God requires is you making the right step in the direction He has called you to. Too many of us believe God wants us to do and get the world before we are qualified for His help. Simply move toward what He has called you to and you will activate His help. Some will walk in the direction, others will run; some creep, while others will crawl. There are some who, because of what life has dealt them, they can only draw toward God. There are those who made it through a life ordeal alive, but the abuse and the trauma from losses and disappointments have left them with a limp. Come with this limp! You are shaking but still move toward that dream. You are afraid of the unknown but keep going. The greatest acts stand on the shoulders of the small efforts made each day toward the desired goals.

AFFIRMATION

One step toward my dream is better than the ten I took running away in fear. If I have enough faith to make the first step, then God, who created the staircase, will hold my hand to cover more ground. He cannot order steps I fail to take, so whether the step is shaky or not, I will make it!

DAY 42

THE DUMPSTER

"When you pass through the waters, I will be with you; and when you pass through the rivers, they will not sweep over you. When you walk through the fire, you will not be burned; the flames will not set you ablaze." (Isaiah 43:2 – NIV).

The dumpster is on the second phase of the long route just after you have gone through the rocky path with low-lying thorns and made it across the river. The dumpster comes after you have already gone through a lot. The dumpster represents the negative energy and words from naysayers. Words are not wind; they are like canine teeth possessing the ability to rip and tear. However, this can only happen if you allow it to.

As the dumpster never changes its position, so naysayers will never change. There will always be talks about whether you can make it or not, whether you are enough or not. The voice of your past will come with the reminder of your mistakes. As you push past the dumpster, covering your nose, push past the stench of the naysaying securing your spirit.

You secure your spirit by intentionally choosing what you pay attention to. The dumpster is another phase that will pass. The dumpster is just another fire that cannot burn you.

AFFIRMATION

Negative words cause some to break, but with the help of God, they are fueling me to break records.

DAY 43

LET THE ROD TALK

"Even though I walk through the darkest valley, I will fear no evil, for you are with me; your rod and your staff, they comfort me." (Psalm 23:4 – NIV).

The rod of God corrects and disciplines, while His staff offers support and guidance. God only corrects who He loves, and even God will not force correction upon anyone because stern discipline awaits those who leave the path. He who hates correction will die. On the course of preparation—the long route—there is always someone looking out to ensure the prescribed path is followed and, oh boy, they are ready to wield the rod of correction. Little did we know that the concept of correction was being infused into our reality because it would play a big part in our development.

Correction is highly resented in today's age because it is viewed as an attack on their person, but here is the comfort in correction: it prevents you from failing in places you were meant to thrive in. Listen to advice and accept corrections and, in the end, you will be wise. Correction is painful, but it is also priceless.

AFFIRMATION

Correction is painful, but it's priceless.

DAY 44

SERVE AND GROW: IMPACT AND GO

"The righteous will flourish like a palm tree, they will grow like a cedar of Lebanon; planted in the house of the LORD, they will flourish in the courts of our God. They will still bear fruit in old age, they will stay fresh and green." (Psalm 92:12-14 – NIV).

Preparation builds you! There are three groups of people you should be mindful of on this journey of life: those who you look up to, those who you are in the same phase with, and those who look up to you. The first class are those who will hold your hands. The second are those who understand your exact circumstances because they are subjected to like conditions, and the third are those who are impacted by your actions or the lack thereof.

The journey is hard because it is designed to build you; hence, the importance of having persons who will hold your hand. While this is great, this, along with the second, are groups that you choose. The third group—those who you impact intentionally or unintentionally—are out of your control to choose.

The third group challenges you to live and live purposely. You cannot choose who looks up to you and, as such, we learn to live in prudence. Preparation puts you in proper perspective on what you are handing down. What impact are you having? What is it that you will be remembered for? Going through the course of preparation is like a seed planted in the soil. It burst open to expose that which will be subjected to death in order to bring life. As the seed defies the phase of the soil, so you will defy all that is challenging your drive to live purposefully. Thereafter, you will flourish and continue to flourish even in your old age. The mind is the biggest barrier between where we are and where we should be, and faith in God can fix this. God can unburden you from the weight of that which is holding you back. All that you need to do well is already in you!

AFFIRMATION

I want, at the end of my walk on this journey of life, to have given all I have to give and impacted all the lives I was born to impact. I am not worthless. I am useful.

DAY 45

TALK GOOD

"The tongue has the power of life and death, and those who love it will eat its fruit." (Proverbs 18:21 – NIV).

When one enters the long route, the sole aim is to get to the end where you can have a home run. Amidst the noise, the naysaying, the distractions, and notwithstanding the resurgence of the past, there is one thing that should remain pure and clean: that is the voice in your head—your voice—what you think of yourself and what you say over yourself.

Shoe cleaning was a very important part of training because deportment is held in high regard. Everyone gets upset when we have to run the long route because not only do we have to get through the journey, but we also have to come back and clean our shoes in preparation for the next session. This we did until it became second nature. Imagine if every time someone or something tries to mess up your mind, you step back and remind yourself of the truth God holds about you. You will become much more resistant to threats that lie ahead.

When everything around you is bad, speak good and watch your atmosphere change. Speak to your identity: *"I am who God says I am. I am strong, courageous, and more than enough."* Speak to your perseverance: *"Better is the end of a thing than the beginning."* Speak to your peace: *"I am secured in God who can settle my soul."* Speak to your process: *"You cannot kill me!"* Speak to your barriers: *"I will overcome."* Speak to your purpose: *"You will not die or be aborted."* Speak to your health: *"I will prosper and be in good health as my soul prospers."* Speak over your family: *"You are giants on the earth."* Speak to your career: *"You will grow from strength to strength."* Speak to your finances: *"God will give me the grace to enlarge my territory."* Speak to your joy: *"You will be preserved."* Speak to your faith: *"I will rise again and as often as I need to."* Speak to the journey: *"I will leave better than I came."*

When you run out of what to say, repeat what God says about you. Talk good!

AFFIRMATION

If I don't have good to say, I have nothing to say.

POEM: 'PREPARATION'

On the back side of the desert, tending sheep that are not mine
In the wilderness of brokenness
This should make sense, but where's the sign?
Gethsemane was chosen for me
Long route given to me
Oh, that I could pass on this!
But darkness of preparation is the light that keeps your purpose well lit.

The palace is ahead, but it's the pit that is in view
High waters flowing
Strong billows rolling
Rolling tides, weeping willows
Isn't this a seaview minus the garden?
Who would have imagined the prep for purpose could be this disheartening
But there is a fellow that eats at your destiny
And it doesn't leave your side
The same power that elevates you will deflate you
Ask Tyrus and he will tell you
To tame the fellow called pride
The process of preparation got this in mind.

The journey appears lonely
So you try to do so much to stay in the light

Truth be told, it's by His Spirit always and never your might.
For your headspace, please fight
Fight and get it right
At His least, our best is vapour
His foolishness is doubly wiser than our greatest wisdom
His weakness is a tower of strength to us
His way we just cannot fathom
Run the long route
The long route you should run.

You are separated, not isolated
Called out, not called off
As you meander through the valley
Remember His rod and His staff
You must be disciplined
So relax, you won't die
In fact, He's guiding you with His loving eye

When He calls you to come away
You are poised for elevation
If you must live by His instructions
You must go through the necessary preparation
Long route!

A CALL TO PRAY:

BE MY GUIDE

Hebrews 4:16 invites me to come boldly before Your throne so I can find grace to help in times of trouble. Great and Sovereign King, I hereby honour Your invitation. Here I am bowed before You! I need Your guidance. May Your hand that guides and corrects never be withdrawn from me. I acknowledge my proclivity to slack off, drift, be distracted and wander away from who You have called be to be. I pray that I will never circumvent the process because it's preparing me for life-changing opportunities.

Increase my faith in You and cause my confidence to be deep rooted in Your truth—the steps of the righteous are ordered by You. May I never run ahead of myself, and I pray that I will make no decision that will abort my purpose.

Dear Jesus, where there is the possibility of me returning to the beggarly elements of my past-addictions, lust, idolatry, injustice, adultery, inordinate affection, lies, unfaithfulness, cursing and curses, apply more grace. Give grace also to thwart the enemy's arrows, neutralize diabolic venoms, disfigure satanic images, and shatter demonic strongholds.

Hold my hands, God, and grant me grace to rise to the task despite fear and insecurities. Guide my feet that I don't take refuge in the camp of the conspirators nor fall into the snare of the fowler. Turn the counsel of liars around for my good.

Great God, dismiss every evil prophesy operating against my life so that I can serve and grow, make and impact and go having left a legacy and created an inheritance for posterity. Cause my speech to edify, educate, correct in love, and connect people that will build healthy empires. Guide my tongue from speaking evil and my lips from speaking guile, in Jesus' Name. Amen.

POEM: 'A NOTE FROM RIBENA'

I sat in the kitchen on an old white chair
Seemingly it has many years
So I knew it was a wise thing to do
Sit still and observe.

My observation led me to notice the Ribena tree
A fraction of its true view as portrayed in a rectangular frame created by the door jam
My eyes jammed upon seeing the tree dancing
Riding flamboyantly the rhythm of the wind
Its leaves striking chords of melody
Its branches putting on display its bunches
Bunches of Ribena riding well the notes of soprano
It's high time they got picked
I never quite understood the song
Until the orchestra crescendoed into silence
A fruit fell to the ground.

No blood spilt
But its impact passed without a note sounding
The fruit riding dub-wise
The rhythm of silence as its voice from the earth sings
If your fruit is not harnessed, it will drop off
Not just off key
But missing its key opportunity to make its impact

Oh, I wish to the call to manifest you would heed
But a message of hope is in every breath that He breathes
Put it on the drums, the keys, the strings
Sound it on the rhythm of the wind
To every nation, every tribe, and every creed
Every fruit, harnessed or smashed
Has within it a seed.

ABOUT THE AUTHOR

Shantel C. Powell also known as the 'Pretty Praying Poetic Police' goes by the theme 'weather the weather whether you want to or not' and this quote as simple as it is has shaped and sharpened her perspective giving light to new possibilities notwithstanding the dark times in which we live.

Shantel C. Powell is a Jesus Girl who has been gifted with wisdom that is primarily expressed in writing. Her writing was acknowledged by the JCDC in 2021 for the award-winning poem *'A note from Ribena'*. Her life can be summarized by the expression of faith forged from adversity. She believes God has placed a message in everything we encounter but only a very few take time to stop, listen, observe and extract; the simple things are indeed our blessing.

Professionally, she is a Police Officer with the Jamaica Constabulary Force and she is dedicated to serving people and is convinced that it is the prayer that pins us to purpose.

www.ingramcontent.com/pod-product-compliance
Lightning Source LLC
Chambersburg PA
CBHW050641160426
43194CB00010B/1757